Adventure Cookery

Teddy, Bears' Picnic

WRITTEN BY
WENDY-ANN ENSOR

ILLUSTRATED BY
WENDY LEWIS

Evans

Evans Brothers Limited

NOTES TO PARENTS AND TEACHERS

The Adventure Cookery series is intended for use at home or at school. All the recipes have been carefully tested both by my own children and in our classroom kitchen.

Each book begins by introducing the theme and setting of the adventure. There are five recipes in each book linked to the adventure theme and which involve weighing and measuring (both metric and imperial measurements are given). The diagrams and simple step-by-step instructions can be followed by a child, although an adult should always help when the oven is to be used or the cooking involves a gas burner or hotplate.

I have found that if an idea catches a child's imagination an associated activity, such as cooking, can operate as a bridge leading to creative writing, art and craft and the practical application of maths and science. These books will, I hope, help you to provide that bridge.

Wendy-Ann Ensor

Before starting to cook

Remember:

1 Wash your hands and make sure your hair is tied back from your face.

2 Put on an apron.

3 Collect everything you need on the table in front of you.

4 Weigh the exact quantities written in the recipe.

5 If you taste the mixture wash your spoon at once.

6 If you spill anything on the floor wipe it up immediately.

Take care

handles   hot dishes

sharp knives   cooker hotplates

About Bears

Bears can be all shapes and sizes and colours.

There are big brown grizzly bears who live in the Rocky Mountains in America.
There are white polar bears who live in the ice and snow and hunt for fish and seals.

There are black bears who hunt for honeycombs in the hollows of trees.

How many different types of bear can you name?

HONEY BUNS

Some bears eat honey by the pawful but that could be rather rich for you and also very sticky! Make some bread rolls and then spread honey on them. Your guests will love these honey buns.

You will need:

450g (1lb) plain flour
1 teaspoon salt
25g (1oz) lard or soft margarine
12.5g (4oz) dried yeast
300ml (½ pint) warm water
1 teaspoon castor sugar
Honey for spreading

What to do:

1 Warm the flour in a mixing bowl.

2 Cream the yeast with a little warm water and the sugar. Leave for 10 minutes.

3 Add the salt to the flour and add in the fat. Pour the yeast and warm water into the centre and mix well with your hands.

4 Lift the dough onto a well-floured board and knead for 5 minutes.

5 Shape the dough into small rolls – it should make 10.

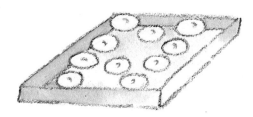

6 Leave the rolls in a warm place until they have doubled in size.

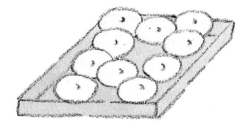

7 Bake in a very hot oven (Reg. 7/425°F/220°C) until they are golden brown.

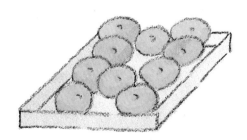

You can eat warm or cold rolls spread with honey at your picnic.

TEDDY PIZZA

Most homes have a teddy bear living in them. Some are as tiny as your middle finger while others may be bigger than you are. You could make a pizza like your teddy bear's face with lovely round ears, two eyes, a nose and a mouth.

You will need:

225g (8oz) plain flour
50g (2oz) margarine
50g (2oz) cooking fat
100g (4oz) grated cheddar cheese
2 large, flat mushrooms
2 slices cucumber
1 strip red pepper
A little water

What to do:

1 Rub the fat into the flour with your fingers until the mixture looks like fine crumbs.

2 Add the water, a little at a time, until you have a firm dough.

3 Put on a floured board and roll lightly.

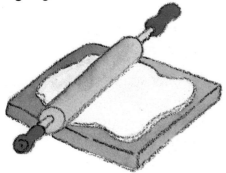

4 Use a plate or saucepan lid to cut your circle.

5 Sprinkle the grated cheese on top.

6 Put 2 mushrooms for ears, 2 slices of cucumber for eyes and a strip of red pepper for the mouth. You could use tomato, sardine or bacon if you would rather eat these.

7 Cook in a hot oven (Reg 6/400°F/ 200°C) for about 20 minutes.

Does your pizza look happy like your own teddy bear?

BEARS' PAWS

Bears' feet are very strong and they have five toes. On each toe they have a long powerful claw which is useful when they are climbing trees. You could make fruit buns to look like bears' paws and add nuts for their claws.

You will need:

450g (1lb) self-raising flour
75g (3oz) margarine
75g (3oz) brown sugar
Paper cake cases
½ teaspoon mixed spice
1 egg
75g (3oz) dried fruit
Milk to mix
A few almonds

What to do:

1 Sieve the flour into a bowl and rub in the fat until the mixture looks like fine crumbs.

2 Add sugar, dried fruit and mixed spice.

3 Mix gradually with enough milk to make a stiff dough.

4 Put a spoonful into each cake case.

Bake in a hot oven (Reg· 7/425°F/ 220°C) for 10 minutes.

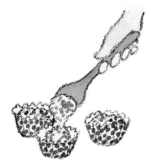

5 Cut your almonds in half lengthways.

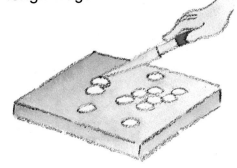

6 Press 5 pieces of almond in each cake for the claws on the bears' paws.

Now you have some brown bears' paws.

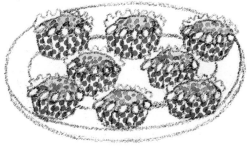

BEARSBERRY FOOL

Black and brown bears eat roots, shoots, honey, fruit and insects. For your picnic you could use some fruit and make a Bearsberry Fool. Your teddy bear will want to share this tasty dish with you.

You will need:

450g (1lb) cooking apples
1 tablespoon custard powder
1 tablespoon castor sugar
275ml (½ pt) milk
Cherries to decorate

What to do:

1 Cut the apples in quarters and peel them. Remove the core.

2 Cook the apples in a little water until they are soft.

3 Beat until smooth with a wooden spoon.

4 Mix the custard powder and sugar slowly with the milk.

5 Cook on a low heat until thick. Remember to stir all the time.

6 Allow this mixture to cool, then stir the custard into the apple.

7 Pour the mixture into bowls or glasses and decorate with cherries.

8 Serve very cold

POLAR PUNCH

Polar bears live in the Arctic regions of the world where it is very, very cold. Their coats are thick and greasy to protect them from the ice and snow. They are excellent swimmers and can make long journeys in the sea without resting on land. Make some refreshing Polar Punch to drink.

You will need:

4 lemons
Ice cubes
A little boiling water
600ml (1 pt) cold water
4 tablespoons castor sugar

What to do:

1 Squeeze the lemons and pour the juice into a jug.

2 Add the sugar and enough boiling water to dissolve it.

3 Fill the jug with cold water.

4 Add the ice cubes. This will look like icebergs in your sea of punch.

If you want to make your drink fizzy you could add a little mineral water.

13

Activity Page

There is a well-known song about teddy bears having a picnic in the woods. Do you know the words?

This is how you can make some trees for your wood.

What to do:

1 Put two sheets of newspaper together and cut halfway down in strips.

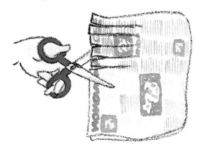

It would be a good idea to have a picnic basket in which to carry your food.

What to do:

You could paint the box.
Make sure it is quite dry before you put food in it **or** you could glue scraps of material over it.

2 Roll up the paper and fasten with sticky tape.
Make as many trees as you think you will need for your wood.

Now you have made all the food for your Teddy Bears' Picnic you can pack it in your picnic hamper and invite your friends to come to the woods. Don't forget to ask them to bring their teddy bears!